NATIONAL GEOGRAPHIC

Ladders

NATIVE AMERICANS OF THE SOUTHEAST

GENRE Social Studies Article

Read to find out how the geography and climate of Florida affected the lives of the Seminole.

THE SEMINOLE OF THE SWAMPS

by Brinda Gupta

Northern and southern states have different **climates**. Climate is the average weather over time. It affects the way you live. If you live in the northern United States, you know how to dress for cold weather. You probably have a closet full of warm clothes. But if you live in the southern part of the country, you might just need a light jacket for winter. Where you live affects how you live, so climate also shaped the lives of early Native Americans.

The Seminole are Native Americans who lived in or migrated to southern Florida's warm climate in the 1700s. The Seminole are a combination of several Native American groups. The mix also includes African Americans who tried to escape slavery. These people all came together and formed a single tribe. The Seminole adapted their lives to the steamy swamps and tropical climate they lived in.

∨ This illustration shows a Seminole family in a dugout canoe. Their canoes were sometimes as long as 30 feet. That was big enough to hold an entire family and all of their belongings.

BEATING THE HEAT

Florida has two climates. Northern Florida has a subtropical climate, which means it has hot, wet summers and mild winters. Southern Florida is hot all year because it has a tropical climate. It gets a lot of rain, including hurricanes. The Seminole and other tribes learned to live in southern Florida despite the extreme weather.

You might think that all Native Americans lived in tipis, or tent homes. Tipis were covered with thick buffalo hides to keep people warm inside. But the Seminole didn't need warm homes. They needed cool and dry homes.

Traditionally, the Seminole lived in huts called *chickees*. Chickees were open on the sides to let breezes blow through. Their thatched roofs protected families from Florida's hot sun and heavy rains. The Seminole built their chickees among **hammocks**, areas of land that rise over grassy swamps. Because the land was so wet and could flood in heavy rain, chickees were raised on stilts to stay dry.

∨ Long ago, the Seminole used local materials to make chickees like this reconstruction. They used wood from cypress trees to make poles that held up the roof. They wove palm fronds, or leaves, together to make the roof. Chickees were easy to build. They stayed cool and dry in the swampland.

TRAVELING THROUGH WETLANDS

The Seminole lived near swamps called the Everglades. To move about the region, they could either walk or canoe. When walking, the Seminole followed animal trails that snaked through the hammocks. For quicker travel, they moved through the waterways in canoes.

The Seminole used special canoes called dugout canoes, which they made from the logs of cypress trees. They used poles to push these flat-bottomed canoes through water. Poles worked better than paddles because the swampy waterways were shallow. The poles allowed canoers to push off the bottom to move along.

The Everglades were full of dangers. Poisonous snakes hid in the grasses, and alligators lurked below the water's surface. Though alligators can travel on land, they spend most of their time in marshes and swamps. The Seminole learned to respect these and other animals. They gave them a lot of space as they canoed through the Everglades.

The Seminole still build dugout canoes. However, the biggest cypress trees were cut down years ago. So modern Seminole canoes are usually smaller than the traditional canoes.

This modern Seminole uses a pole to push his dugout canoe. The ancestors of the Seminole made and used dugout canoes as far back as 5,000 years ago.

FISH AND FRUIT

The Seminole got much of their food from the waterways. Standing in their canoes, they speared fish. They collected snails and oysters from the water. A Seminole brave enough to hunt an alligator could make a meal from its cooked meat. In forests nearby, the Seminole hunted animals such as deer, rabbits, and turkeys.

The region's climate could be uncomfortably sticky. But it was perfect for picking wild berries and growing other fruits and vegetables such as beans and squash. The Seminole ate pumpkins, pineapples, and oranges, and they grew corn and sugarcane. A Seminole meal may have included roasted fish with wild rice and sweet potatoes, cornbread, and a fruit salad of bananas and grapes. In their climate, the Seminole had to live through some hot days, but they would never run out of food.

HEALTHY EATERS

The Seminole had a delicious and varied diet. Corn and flour made from ground corn were ingredients in many of their meals. Even some of their drinks contained corn. They also ate a lot of veggies, like the yellow squash and green beans shown in this photo.

This Seminole woman uses a traditional wooden tool to grind corn for cooking. The tool is called a mortar and pestle. The mortar is the container where the corn is ground. The pestle is the large pole she is using to grind the corn.

Check In How did the Seminole adapt to living in the tropical climate of southern Florida?

Life in a Cherokee VILLAGE

by Becky Manfredini   illustrated by James Madsen

Each Cherokee family had a summer and a winter home. Summer homes were large and rectangular, open and airy. Winter homes were small and round, built to keep the family warm.

The Cherokee lived in large family groups called **clans**. There were seven clans in each tribe: Long Hair, Paint, Bird, Wolf, Wild Potato, Deer, and Blue. The clans have had those names for at least 500 years.

Imagine living beside a river in the region we now know as the states of Georgia, Tennessee, North Carolina, and South Carolina. There are forests of maple, hickory, and pine trees all around you. Your home is one of 40 in a village in which more than 400 people live. You do your chores and then play games with other children while your mother plants corn and your father carves hunting tools.

That's what life was like for the Cherokee people. The Cherokee are a Native American people who lived in the foothills of the Appalachian Mountains in the southeastern United States. Foothills are the low parts of a mountain range. Some Cherokee still live in this region. But most Cherokee were forced by the U.S. government to move west during the 1830s.

Each Cherokee village had a **plaza**, or public square, in its center. The plaza was used for meetings, trading, and religious ceremonies.

Home and Hearth

Cherokee villages were full of activity from sunrise to sunset all through the year. The Cherokee farmed in summer and hunted in winter. Men cleared the fields to plant crops, but women grew the food. Boys wrestled, played games, and imitated their fathers' hunting skills by using small bows and arrows to shoot at squirrels and rabbits. Girls helped their mothers with chores and learned to run a household.

Cherokee women ground corn into flour or added it to soups. They made clothing by sewing pieces of animal skins together with needles made from animal bones. The women raised the children of the village together.

Cherokee women were the owners of the land. They planted and harvested corn, squash, and beans.

CHEROKEE VILLAGE

Men built canoes and the village's buildings. They also helped with the harvest.

In winter, the men left to hunt deer, turkey, and bear. The Cherokee used every part of these animals. They ate the deer meat, and they made clothing from the skin and tools from the antlers and bones.

Cherokee men used axes with blades made of stone and handles made of bone to cut down trees. They built dugout canoes from the tree trunks. To make the canoes, they burned out the logs' centers and then scraped away the charred wood.

The Cherokee caught fish with **weirs**, which were underwater traps made of stone and branches. They also fished using bows and arrows, spears, and nets.

By the Water

The Cherokee built their villages near rivers and lakes, so they could more easily get water for drinking, cooking, and bathing. The men caught fish. The women prepared and cooked the fish. The waterways also gave them a way to travel in canoes to trade goods. When Europeans moved onto their land, the Cherokee began to trade their deerskins for the Europeans' metal tools, guns, glass, and cloth.

CHEROKEE VILLAGE

Water wasn't used only for serious purposes. Cherokee children loved to swim, splash around, and cool off.

Cherokee women gathered reeds, or the tall grasses that grew along the rivers, to make baskets. The baskets were used for storing and carrying food and firewood.

In the Plaza

Today, people go to malls, theaters, and grocery stores to buy things they need and to see friends. For the Cherokee, the plaza was *the* place to be. The Cherokee came there to spend time together, hold meetings, dance, and celebrate.

On holidays, the Cherokee lit a fire in the plaza to celebrate with friends and neighbors. A person called the Firekeeper kept the fire burning throughout the holiday.

The Council House was a large circular building in the plaza where the Cherokee held meetings. Villagers sat on benches along the walls to hear the elder Cherokee women and men have discussions and make decisions. One important village decision might be whether or not to go to war.

At sundown during holidays, people in the plaza did the Stomp Dance. The Stomp Dance is a religious and social dance that has been part of Cherokee life for hundreds of years. People called shell shakers shake rattles made of pebbles and turtle shells they wear on their legs. They make a rhythm by shuffling their feet. The dancers circle the fire, dancing to the rhythm.

Check In   What types of work did men and women do in a traditional Cherokee village?

Se

quoyah

by Sheri Reda

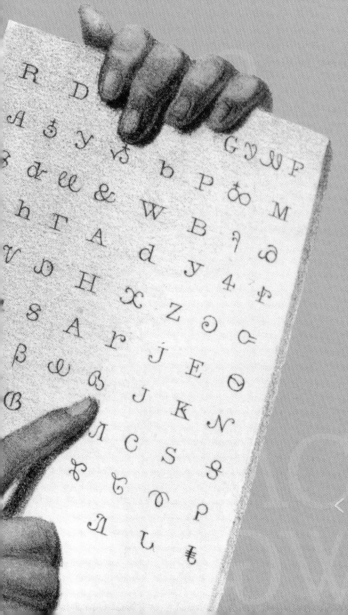

Sequoyah (sih-KWOY-yuh) was a Cherokee leader who actually had two names. Sequoyah was his Cherokee name, and George Guess was his English name. Because his father was a white trader and his mother was Cherokee, Sequoyah grew up in two cultures. Yet he came to be respected by all. Sequoyah was so highly honored that the tallest, strongest trees in the country were named after him.

Sequoyah was born in the Cherokee village of Taskigi in central Tennessee, sometime between 1760 and 1775. He and two brothers were raised by their mother. He became a trader and a **silversmith**. A silversmith makes forks, knives, jewelry, and other items out of silver and other metals.

Sequoyah fought in the U.S. Army during the Creek War of 1813–1814. That conflict was fought mainly between Native American tribes, but the United States also took part in it. This event changed Sequoyah's life. Keep reading to find out how.

Sequoyah sat for this portrait during a visit to Washington, D.C. He came to Washington, D.C., to sign a peace treaty between the Cherokee people and the U.S. government.

The Inventor

When he was in the army, Sequoyah saw American soldiers writing letters, reading orders, and recording events. He came to believe that the secret to the Americans' power was writing. At that time, the Cherokee had no written language, so most of their knowledge depended on word of mouth and memorization. Sequoyah shared his idea about creating a written Cherokee language with some friends. They were doubtful, but he couldn't forget the idea.

After leaving the army, Sequoyah got married and had a family, but he remained interested in writing. Sequoyah knew that Native Americans had rich cultures, and they passed their cultures down to younger generations by telling stories. He also knew that writing was an easier way to preserve information for future generations.

Sequoyah first attempted to create a written Cherokee language in 1809. He created a symbol for each Cherokee word, but there were too many symbols to remember. Stumped, Sequoyah asked his daughter Ayoka for help. Together, they identified 85 different sounds in the Cherokee language. Then Sequoyah created a symbol for each of the sounds. Finally, he combined the symbols into words, and that worked.

Sequoyah's writing system is called a syllabary (SIH-luh-bur-ee) because each symbol stands for a syllable in the Cherokee language. In English, each symbol stands for a letter.

DWℰG

< SHOE
The Cherokee word for shoe is *alasulo* (ah-lah-SOO-lo), but moccasins like these are *tsulawa* (tsoo-LAH-wah).

ᎤᎵᏌᎤᎤ

> TURTLE
Do you think that this eastern box turtle knows that it's called a *daksi* (DAHK-see) in Cherokee?

WMC

> BASKET
The Cherokee word for basket is *talutsi* (tah-LOO-tsee). This traditional basket is woven from honeysuckle vine.

DCЈ

< FISH
One Cherokee word for fish is *atsadi* (aht-SAHD-ee). They also have words for different kinds of fish. A trout is an *uga* (OO-GAH).

The Legacy

In 1821, Sequoyah and his daughter had to defend their writing system before the Cherokee Tribal Council, which thought the system might be "witchcraft." Council members placed Sequoyah and Ayoka in separate rooms. They had Sequoyah write a message and then brought it to Ayoka, who read and answered Sequoyah's message. The two continued to exchange messages quickly, with no errors.

Council members were impressed and could see that there was no magic involved. They approved the writing system and even asked to learn it themselves. Within a week, the council learned to read and write Cherokee. Within months, much of the

ᏇE
TREE

Sequoia trees grow to heights of 300 feet or more. That's about the height of the Statue of Liberty or a 30-story building.

300 ft

200 ft

100 ft

Cherokee nation could read and write in its own language.

In 1825, the Cherokee honored Sequoyah with a silver medal and a lifetime **salary**. But he continued working. He published a newspaper in Cherokee and English. In 1828, the *Cherokee Phoenix* became the first newspaper printed in a Native American language.

When Sequoyah died in 1843, people all over the world shared the Cherokee's sadness. He gave the gifts of reading and writing to the Cherokee. He also gave the gift of Cherokee stories to the world.

> More than ten years after Sequoyah's death, a scientist honored him by naming the giant California redwood trees after him. Sequoyah's great deeds truly made him a "giant."

PIECES
of the Past

by Becky Manfredini

illustrated by Suling Wang

You're hiking along a trail when you discover bits of broken pottery. You pick up these **shards** and wonder where they came from. You also wonder who used them and for what purpose. You think about how the shards got here on the trail. If you enjoy putting together pieces of a puzzle like this, you might like to learn about **archaeology** (ahr-kee-OL-uh-jee). Archaeologists study artifacts, or objects from the past, to learn how people lived long ago.

About 4,000 years ago, Native Americans of the Southeast began making pottery. Over time, different Native American tribes developed their own styles of pottery and decorations, which they painted on the pottery.

> Archaeologists collected all the shards shown below. Then they pieced them together to reveal the original form of a pot.

< If you saw these shards, how would you know they were pieces of broken pottery? Archaeologists look at the edges and the pattern on the shard to be sure it was from a pot and not just a rock.

From the Earth

Native Americans of long ago used pottery for many purposes. They needed containers for storing, cooking, and serving food and drinks. They gave pottery as gifts. They also used pottery for religious reasons, sometimes as offerings for the dead.

If you've ever made a piece of pottery, you know that it's made of clay, a sticky kind of earth. Clay is soft when it's wet, and you can easily shape it. It hardens when it dries or when you bake it in a special oven. Native American potters **tempered** the clay, or made it stronger, by mixing it with other materials. For example, people on the coast used crushed shells or sand to temper their pots. Potters near the forest used crushed animal bones. People near streams and rivers used pebbles. Some potters used crushed shards from old pots to temper new pots.

< Native Americans of the Southeast still make pottery today. Some tribes decorate their work with patterns. Other tribes carve or paint animals or people onto the pottery.

Pottery People

Thousands of years ago, Native American pottery makers lived in many tribes throughout the land that is now the southeastern United States. Each tribe's pottery style was unique to its culture.

< Native American potter Sweeny Willis made this pot using a coiling method.

Mississippian

Mississippian people lived near the Mississippi River. They painted and carved designs on clay jars, plates, and pots. They also made pots in the shape of a human head. They left these pots as offerings when they buried their dead. Archaeologists have found these pots in Arkansas and Missouri. They date back to about A.D. 700.

> This Mississippian pitcher was crafted into the form of a woman with a tattooed face.

∨ This Pamunkey bowl was made in the early 1900s. It represents a man wearing a feather headdress.

Pamunkey

The Pamunkey tribe of northeastern Virginia began trading pottery to European settlers in the 1600s. Their pottery was made with river clay that was rich and dark. Besides pottery for table use, the Pamunkey made bowls, pipes, and other containers.

Cherokee

Almost 2,000 years ago, the Cherokee of Tennessee and North Carolina began a unique tradition called "stamped pottery." Potters stamped their pottery using wooden paddles that had designs carved into them. The designs were transferred into the clay.

> A modern-day Cherokee artist crafted this stamped pottery.

Catawba

For thousands of years, the Catawba of South and North Carolina have made pottery of dark clay. Depending on the kind of wood put in the fires to bake the pottery, the pieces are streaked with beige, brown, or gray. Some Catawba potters make bowls in the shape of snakes, birds, and squirrels.

∧ The modern Catawba artist who made this beaver polished it to make it shine.

∨ This modern streaked Catawba vessel features a human face.

Making Pottery

If you lived thousands of years ago, here's how you might have made
a container to hold water or food.

1 **SOFTEN THE CLAY:** Prepare a lump of clay for shaping. Add water. Then **knead** it, or work it with your hands, until it's soft enough to shape.

2 **TEMPER:** Add a handful of pebbles, sand, or crushed shells.

5 **SMOOTH:** Use your fingers to smooth the sides of the container, inside and out.

6 **DRY:** Place your clay object in the hot sun to dry it. Depending on how dry or humid the air is, this step could take up to two weeks!

3 **ROLL:** Make smaller lumps of clay. Roll each one into a long coil.

4 **FORM AND STACK:** Form the coils into circles. Stack the circles on top of each other to form a container.

7 **PAINT:** Paint a design on it that tells something about your culture, or way of life.

8 **BAKE:** Put your object in a kiln, or pottery oven. When it's dry, you will have your own piece of pottery.

Check In What is the most interesting information you've learned about the pottery of the southeastern Native Americans?

Discuss

1. What connections can you make among the four selections in this book? How do you think the selections are related?

2. How do you think the writing system that Sequoyah invented would benefit the Cherokee?

3. Describe the traditional Cherokee way of life, including their jobs, pastimes, and community events. How does the Cherokee way of life of long ago compare to your life today?

4. What can archaeologists learn about Native Americans of the Southeast by studying shards of broken pottery?

5. What would you still like to find out about the Native Americans of the Southeast?